SOARING EAGLES

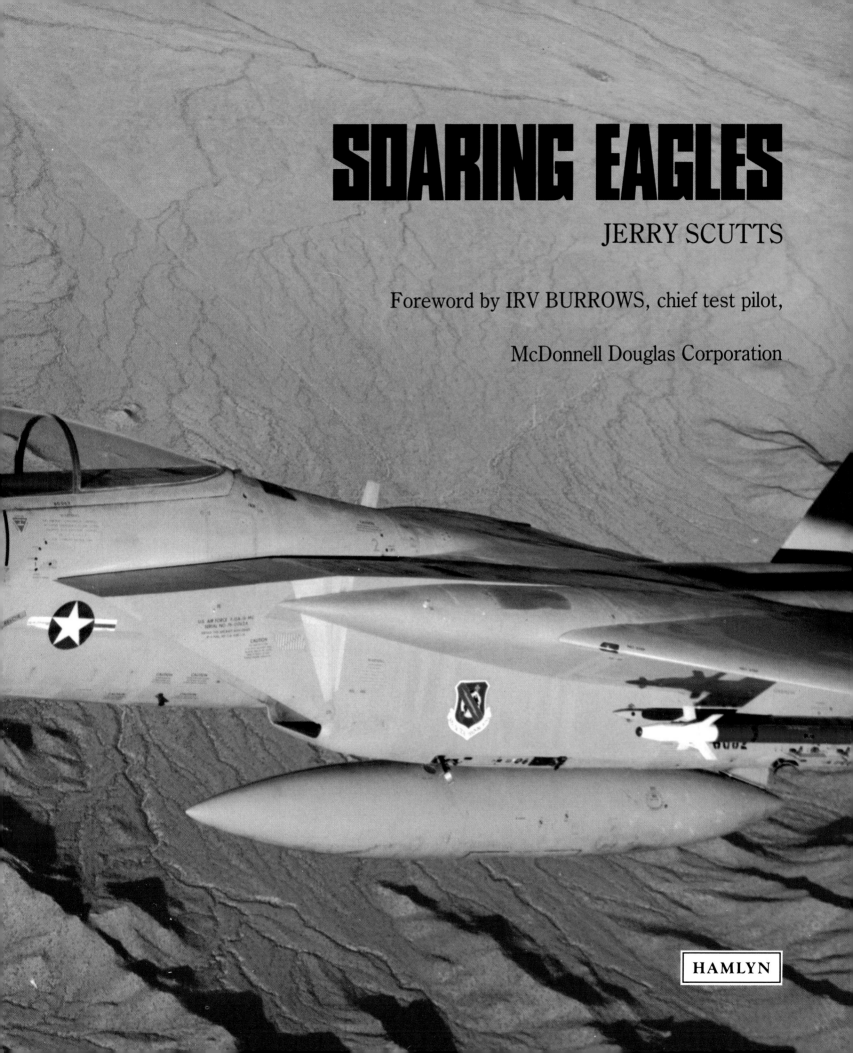

SOARING EAGLES

JERRY SCUTTS

Foreword by IRV BURROWS, chief test pilot,

McDonnell Douglas Corporation

HAMLYN

First published in 1990 by The Hamlyn Publishing Group,
a division of The Octopus Publishing Group Ltd
Michelin House, 81 Fulham Road, London SW3 6RB

Copyright © The Hamlyn Publishing Group 1990

Photographs © McDonnell Douglas, except as below

Typeset by SX Composing Ltd, Rayleigh, Essex

ISBN 0600 568 27X

Additional photographs © George Hall/Check Six pp62-65, 90-91, 96, 106-109, 116-117, 130-131 and 142-143; Patrick Allen pp110-111.
The Publishers are grateful to Geoffrey Norris of McDonnell Douglas, Europe and Tim Beecher,
Director of Communications, McDonnell Douglas Corporation, St Louis, Miss
for their help in compiling this book.

Produced by Mandarin Offset
Printed and bound in Hong Kong

FOREWORD

This plane feels like a real fighter I thought, as I hauled her thru some tight G turns. She performed without a hitch leaving my chase plane staggering around in the clouds way below me.

Taking off in the F-15 is a unique experience and no matter how many times that you do it you are deeply respectful of the plane under your control. The Eagle has been very aptly named.

Pete Garrison and I logged up over forty hours of test flying prior to delivering the F-15 over to the USAF for further testing. After full evaluation by them the first production aircraft rolled off the production line some eleven months after I took the first prototype up. It seemed like a flawless scenario.

Today the F-15 has reached the E varient. This aircraft has now gone into squadron service and we are well into development programs relating to STOL. In spite of fiscal problems in Congress the F-15 program looks well set for the 21st Century.

Irv Burrows
Washington, D.C.

INTRODUCTION

Eagle – symbol of America – for the new McDonnell Douglas fighter to succeed the Phantom, it was a name that seemed to do nicely. In 1969 the FX program aimed at an F-4 replacement for the US Air Force was won by McDonnell Douglas, but bettering the Phantom represented a huge investment, a king-size job.

Building a fighter that would fully meet the FX specification meant adapting the best of aeronautical technology. Little expense was spared and when the new aircraft was unveiled, nobody saw any problem in naming it after nature's king of birds. The F-15 Eagle was born.

People who thought the Phantom big for a fighter – which had two seats – were in for a shock. Not only was the F-15 larger still, they'd put one man back in the cockpit.

Spanning just over 42 feet with a needle-nosed, twin-finned fuselage that was nearly a foot longer than the F-4E, the Eagle may just have looked too much for one pilot to handle. Such a view was not in tune with modern electronic capabilities, as was soon to be shown.

Size alone doesn't count for much in the modern fighter business. The F-15 was large because space was needed for a multiple missile load, a big gun and many black boxes. A healthy fuel tankage for the most powerful turbofan engines available also eat up space and a big wing was obviously needed to lift it all and propel it through the sky faster than virtually anything else in the world. More importantly, the bat-winged Eagle was as agile as they came and better than most.

Big did not though, mean too heavy.

The F-15A weighed only eighty per cent as much as a fully loaded F-4, was less complex and far easier to maintain. To the delight of the long-suffering knuckle buster on the groundcrew, there were 300 per cent more access panels than the Phantom had.

Designed into the Eagle was ultimate pilot confidence – the man at the controls would know that even if an enemy fighter did get on his tail, he wouldn't be able to stay there.

Actual combat has shown that one-missile kills are rare. Two, three or more might be needed. Erring on the safe side, McDonnell Douglas gave the Eagle room for eight: four Sparrows are standard, with up to a quartet of Sidewinders, as required. In the Eagle, the dog fighter's fighter was back, with air superiority the only game in town.

Ever since Korea, Russian fighters have been the yardstick against which US combat aircraft design stood or fell. And the Soviets had a significant hand in the size of the F-15 when they started the trend toward big fighters – or so it was believed. In July '67 a MiG-25 Foxbat captured some significant flight records. Western experts jumped to the conclusion that a new era in fighter design had begun.

When the Foxbat turned out not to be the potential threat it was feared, the die for the F-15 was already cast. Even if American aircraft were now unlikely to meet hordes of the big MiGs with swords drawn over some future battlefront, it was kind of reassuring that the US had with the Eagle, taken a few strides forward.

The Eagle project came together on 26

June 1972 when the first example was rolled out of the company's doors at St Louis. On 27 July it was at Edwards Air Force Base, California, scene of so many previous first flights – and not a few shattered hopes. That summer day saw no tears for McDonnell Douglas. Chief test pilot Irv Burrows' maiden flight in the F-15A showed how well the plant technicians had turned raw computer data into a sleek fighting machine. The F-15 flew as good as it looked.

In the next half decade, the company

was to deliver some 450 Eagles, making numerous improvements in the light of extensive test flying and Air Force evaluation. Among the 'fixes' early on was a much larger dorsal speed brake. As no braking 'chute was fitted, F-15 pilots sometimes experienced landing problems, particularly in a cross wind. At typically steep approach angles, air could build up under that big wing and provide lift when it was least needed. Battering the airflow with a barn door of a brake increased to 31 square feet, helped a safe three-pointer to be made.

Early in the development program, the F-15 was also given a second seat. Examples number eight and ten were TF-15As, later redesignated Eagle Bravo. The first production aircraft was in fact a two-seat 'tub'. Handy aircraft for transition training, the F-15Bs were also well employed on trips for the top brass, and other VIPs.

In 1974 General Robert Dixon, then head of Tactical Air Command, made his first Eagle flight. A veteran of combat in three wars, Gen Dixon was more than able to sort a fighter worthy of the name from a lemon. He wasn't to be disappointed by the F-15.

What most impressed the general was the Eagle's long range eye, its Hughes radar. His comment was:

'You can see so far, so well that you're almost all-seeing. A radar that's 10 miles or 20 miles is a relative miracle. But a radar that's 50 miles – up, down or sideways – is almost a brain.'

Riding with Col Wendell Shawler, F-15 flight test director at Edwards, Gen Dixon summed up his sortie with these words:

'The F-15 is as good as there is. I don't know of anything I'd rather have.'

More brass flights followed. Brig Gen Chuck Yeager took a TF-15 up for an hour-long wring out to, as he put it, 'be brought up to date on some new stuff.' Shortly before he retired from the Air Force the man who had first broken the sound barrier said of the F-15, 'Very impressive. Everything works good.' Coming from a pilot with Yeager's experience those simple words meant more than a string of superlatives from a youngster with far fewer entries in his log book.

Production Eagles for the Air Force looked a little different to the hard working test aircraft, of which there were 20. In a unique blue-gray paint scheme, each F-15A had a saw-tooth leading edge to the stabilators to overcome flutter and the original wingtips were clipped back to a steeper angle to eliminate buffeting. No slats or other manoeuvring devices marred the wing line.

In November 1974 Gerald Ford gave Presidential approval to the F-15 program at the handover ceremony to the Air Force at Luke AFB, Arizona. Ahead lay a year of tailoring the F-15 for regular USAF front line service by the 58th Tac Training Wing. When the first Eagle instructors and ground crews

had completed their courses at Luke, Eagle squadrons were ready to multiply. In January 1976 the spotlight turned on Langley, Virginia where the 1st Tactical Fighter Wing became the first operation F-15 unit.

McDonnell Douglas meanwhile turned its attention to recapturing those time-to-climb records set by the MiG-25 and its own Phantom. After all, the company now

had a fighter with a thrust-to-weight ratio better than 1:1. With a little tinkering it could be made to grab sky faster than a Saturn V booster.

For the record attempt, production Eagle number 19 was pulled from the line and stripped down. Out went all non-essential military items to save weight, including the paint. That alone saved 40 pounds. Paint was used only to apply an eagle's head and the name 'Streak Eagle' in red, white and blue across the nose.

To achieve record marks, it was necessary to run the engines of this bald Eagle up to full power before it moved. Asking the brakes to hold back 50,000 pounds of thrust in full 'burner was unrealistic – she'd just slide, melting the tires as she went. So they tethered her to the runway by a cable in place of the standard tailhook.

After McDonnell Chief Experimental Test Pilot Pete Garrison proved that an Eagle lightened by 2800 pounds could climb better than the proverbial bat out of hell, Air Force pilots Willard Macfarlane, Roger Smith and Dave Peterson undertook the actual record attempt. It was no picnic. Each man wore an astronaut's pressure suit, so great would be the G forces imposed; they'd barely have enough fuel for any deviation in the 'straight up' flight plan, and all flights would be on instruments. For the required record-smashing performance, Streak Eagle would have to be held at sustained G loads for the better part of each climb.

On 16 January 1975 Streak Eagle hurtled into the gray North Dakota skies over Grand Forks Air Force Base on the first record attempt. Maj Smith was at the controls; his aim was to shatter the time to 3,000 meters, then held by an F-4 at 34.5 seconds. Smith did it in 27.6. Eight time-to-climb records were quickly broken under official FAI jurisdiction. Roger Smith flew three and Majors Macfarlane and Peterson three and two respectively. The highest altitude was 30,000 meters, or 98,425 feet. On 1 February this one also fell to Major Smith who hit Mach 1 in level flight two minutes after brakes off. Sheer momentum took Streak Eagle on up to 102,000 feet.

These new records, though short-lived, were a fitting culmination of the initial F-15 test phase. They pointed up further improvements to service Eagles and had therefore, lasting value. Resulting modifications included those to the variable geometry engine inlets to improve supersonic performance, plus better pressurisation and fuel flow management.

Like any military pilot the F-15 driver gets a thorough pre-flight briefing as to what he will do on the flight, where he will go in company with how many other aircraft, whether simulated combat will occur and 101 other need-to-know items delivered by the flight leader in a roll-call of jargon and abbreviated terminology baffling to the layman. A modern departure after the briefing – as would definitely be noticed by pilots used to fighters of a bygone age – is that the F-15 pilot then explains all this procedure to his aircraft.

He doesn't, as yet, actually talk to it, but keys it all into the on-board computer, the crucial link between man and machine. The Inertial Navigation System digests details from start point to en-route flight, mission exercise area, entry and egress points and rendezvous points – everything necessary is punched in.

Check flight controls, speed brake and flaps, turn on the air conditioning and our pilot is ready to roll. As it starts to move, the Eagle has to be carefully handled. As the F100 turbofans wind up they create a great deal of unused power. Any ham-fistedness now and the aircraft could unleash itself.

Ordnance is carried on most flights and the pilot rolls to the last chance pit where ground men unholster the missiles or arm the bombs. They hold aloft a bunch of safety pins to show the pilot he is ready to fight. A last minute check for fuel or hydraulic leaks and the Eagle is waved away by the ground crew. From here on in, the pilot's on his own; one man, one airplane.

For this hypothetical flight we can make that most dramatic of F-15 take-offs, the Viking Departure. The pilot brings the engines up to full military power, releases the brakes and pulls back on the stick. The Eagle GOES.

Nose angled up 60 degrees, the F-15 shoots up into the wild blue. With so much power-to-weight under the pilot's hand it can reach Mach 1 going straight up, leaving almost everything else on wings chasing vapour.

Such a mind-numbing sight might convey the impression that those electronic guardian angels and fingertip power control reduce the degree of necessary pilot training. Nothing could be further from the truth. Few members of the F-15 community would deny that a man needs stratospherically high skill, off-the-scale IQ and one hell of a lot of experience, not to mention the reflexes of a cornered wildcat, to usefully occupy an Eagle seat. Only the best get to throw 30 million dollars-worth of hardware around the sky in the knowledge

that all their training could one day be put to the ultimate test of combat for real.

The most demanding part of the mission is ahead. While the F-15 has undeniably been made easy to fly thanks largely to the computer interface between the pilot's flight commands and actual movement of the wing and tail surfaces, nobody can design-out the skill of other pilots briefed to get the drop on him over the ranges. Kill or be killed is what fighter flying is all about.

A disadvantage of the F-15 in air combat manoeuvring is its size. It is reckoned to be seen earlier than the smaller types pitted against it. And an F-15's radar cannot see directly behind. For this reason, a great deal of time is spent on human eye-

ball work. A large Head-Up Display coupled with HOTAS – Hands On Throttle And Stick – control, enables the pilot to continually scan the sky and react to the threat in time.

In an aircraft that can withstand up to 9G in turns and lose or gain thousands of feet of altitude in mere seconds, the pilot's day can still go badly if he is jumped and 'destroyed.'

Simulated air combat often involves the Aggressors, the US instructor pilots who plan, think and fly like Russians. It is their job, using Soviet-style formations and tactics, to jump squadron pilots and theoretically knock them down, using every trick in the book – and a few yet to be written. Sometimes the only realisation that a pilot has lost the game for today is a whoop over the radio. Maybe they got you with a 'Fox One' (Sparrow shot) or 'Fox Two' (Sidewinder) – or even worse 'Fox Three' – guns. Then, the fighter that shot you down was very close indeed and if you still didn't pick him up . . . the post-mission analysis will have to be swallowed and learned from, so that next time, things will be different. Maybe.

By 1979 McDonnell had refined both A and B model Eagles into the F-15C and D respectively. Very similar to the earlier versions, most of the improvements were under the skin. Each model had space for 2,000 pounds more fuel and was able to have FAST – Fuel And Sensor Tactical – packs attached. These ingenious figure-hugging pallets clamp alongside each engine nacelle and boost the F-15's range to 3,450 miles, hardly without imparing performance. They do of course make the aircraft heavier, but when fuel is burned at the rate of 100 gallons a minute if it flies at Mach 1 at 40,000 feet, or an enormous 410 gallons a minute above the speed of sound at sea level, extra fuel is useful. It is also more economical, particularly on time, if fighters can fly further without the need to take on fuel from a tanker.

FAST packs also accommodate weapons on their lower edges, as they otherwise mask the standard 'corner' mountings for the four AIM-7 Sparrows. Alternatively bombs can be hung on the pallets in what is known as tangential carriage, the stub pylons taking up to 12×1,000 lb or four 2,000 lb bombs.

The idea of the F-15 hauling bombs was anathema to fighter pilots. They saw 'their' F-15 as an air-to-air fighter, nothing more. Single seat Eagle drivers fiercely defend their aerial Ferrari, scorning those unfortunate souls – as they see it – whose lot it is to attack ground targets.

Bombs had been carried as early as 1973, and matched to the conformal pallets a year later – but the subsequent combination proved to be the most effective for 'attack' Eagles. The beauty of the FAST pack is that any fuel tradeoff that would have had to be made in a standard F-15 when carrying ordnance is more than made up for – in fact range is actually increased by up to 40 per cent.

As well as a very full attack fighter test program, the company developed significant updates for the F-15C and D, which began to replace older models in the late 1970s. Among the changes were a better ejector seat, the Aces II, which allows for emergency departure from the F-15 flying in any attitude, including inverted; more capable radar and a strengthened airframe and landing gear. Such updates, known as MSIP – Multi-Stage Improvement Program – cover periodic modernisation, carried out as long as aircraft in the service fleet have useful airframe life.

Deliveries of MSIP F-15s began in June 1985 and that same year Air National Guard units received a number of older A and B model aircraft, the first being the 159th Tactical Fighter Group based at New Orleans. As of spring 1989, the active F-15 inventory in the Air Force was 718, with another 99 on flying status with the ANG.

Jerry Scutts
September 1989

Big though this airplane is, it's a lot lighter than the old Phantom. This is due partly to the amount of composites and titanium plus a rationalisation of those black boxes, control devices and instruments that we have installed . . . Did you know that the F-15 is a foot longer and has four feet more wing span than the F-4 yet it weighs in at 20 per cent less when combat ready?

McDonnell Douglas design engineer

These early test machines had some good paint jobs done on them. They really made the plane stand out. That after all, was the reason for painting them in the first place. Each prototype was slightly different – gray with yellow wing and rudder flashes, overall white with blue trim. There was, I remember an overall Air Superiority Blue – that really stood out! Red and white was the favorite combination though.

McDonnell Douglas engineer

That old F-15B demonstrator ship has sure clocked up the miles, showing off the Eagle to the service and VIPs all over the States. In its time, it's carried all the F-15 weapons and now it flies dressed up as the ultra-capable Echo model with all the electronics and ordance we're putting into the two-seat attack model for the 1990s. Best part is that it is also a pretty good dogfighter – but don't let the single-seat Eagle drivers hear you say that!

McDonnell Douglas pilot

We still paint airplanes in different colors, despite the fact that a good radar can pick up anything with a non-Stealth signature. But for peace games, for Europe at least, we've gone 'lizard' which is far easier to say than European One camouflage scheme!

F-15 Ground crew chief

Tanks are still a major battlefield weapon, despite all the air ordnance everybody's got to knock 'em out. The Air Force reckons that the snub-nose Rockeye takes a lot of beating in this role. It's actually a Navy weapon that we've adapted for use on our tactical airplanes. The brochure calls it an 'area denial cluster weapon'. This means that every one of those big bombs splits open and showers out anti-personnel bomblets (717 of them). Rockeyes will also take out light structures and vehicles as well as tanks. The F-15'll carry 22. Guess that should be enough . . .

F-15 navigator

People say that mud mover airplanes are outdated. But when you have a very precise system for getting the airplane to the target and dropping the bombs right where they're meant to go, I can't see the grunts complaining too much. Remember they're the ones who take territory and traditionally, win most of the wars. The F-15 can definitely help them do that.

F-15 Pilot

As a 4th Tactical Fighter Wing backseater who has just converted to the F-15E, I've flown some practise missions using the Pave Tack infra-red laser scanner. You wouldn't believe the accuracy we can achieve with that thing. You don't find many fighters that are as at home down in the weeds as they are at 50,000 feet, but the F-15 is. As the company might say, the Eagle is still pushing at the edge of the flight envelope for this-type airplane. What I also like is that we can be fighter pilots too – we don't, with our load of AAMs as well as ordnance, just have to sit there if we're attacked by enemy fighters.

F-15 Navigator

In fast air combat manoeuvring, the sheer speed at which everything happens in the F-15 can give some inexperienced guys problems. I try to make sure they can hack it. Spatial disorientation is one to watch. I tell them to remember that brown is always down, and blue should be everywhere above the horizon. Call in and get directions from the rest of your element, check your instruments and get within the window for the autopilot; turn it back on and get your gyros uncaged and you should be OK.

The great thing with the Eagle is that you should be able to forget about flying the airplane and concentrate on staying mission-sharp at all times. But if it all comes apart and staying with it is going to ruin your entire day, the Aces II seat has high reliability. Fatalities among guys who've had to jump are far below one percent.

F-15 Pilot

It's a prime consideration for us to be in a fast turn round situation when you're on the front line. Accessibility in this airplane couldn't be better – it's got over 300 access points. Servicing the 20mm Vulcan gun is easy, normally . . .

USAF Senior Master Sergeant

The F-15 is now getting the AIM-120A, the Hughes Advanced Medium Range Air-to-Air Missile or AMRAAM. Designed to replace the Sparrows the Eagle has carried up till now, the '120 is what they call a 'fire and forget' missile with a radar seeker head that only activates when it's near the target. It only weighs a little more than an AIM-9 and it should increase our capability plenty.

F-15 Ground crew chief

Out on regular patrol over Alaska is a wonderfully scenic experience. It is one of the worlds most beautiful places . . . it's just awesome in its grandeur . . . that is when the weather is good. When it is nasty it's sheer hell both up here and on the ground.

F-15 Pilot from 43 TFS,

Alaskan Air Command

As the first F-15 air defense squadron we feel kinda obliged to stay real sharp, ready in case anyone should challenge our slice of the US skies. Missile shoots are a big part of that. Our nickname, 'Tazlanglian Devils' was a 'natural' as our base is Langley, Virginia. Try it a few times, you'll get it. If not, 48th Fighter Interceptor Squadron will do.

F-15 Squadron commander

Dedicated? I would say that we're addicted rather than dedicated. To us the air defense mission is *the* place to be in a US-based F-15 squadron, second only to a tour in USAFE. I don't know of any Eagle pilots who'd trade places with anyone in the Air Force because the F-15 is by a big margin, the best the 318th – or anyone else – has ever had. You should feel that baby climb. It's a real good feeling to leave every other airplane we have way back in our slipstream . . .

My pilots eat, sleep and breathe air-to-air because everyone thinks that if war breaks out anywhere, it's enemy fighters we'd be in combat with, not bombers as they planned for back in the 50s. We know we're better trained today, because that one mission is all we do. Had we had the F-15 in Vietnam and more importantly, pilots trained like today's, the thinking is that the Air Force woulda had a lot more aces. A lot of things point to that being true – and it's not just surmise. A lot of our guys saw combat in 'Nam in F-4s and they know how much of an advance the F-15 is. Compared to today, the fighter pilot of the 1960s hadn't even begun to train for true air-to-air. They were not taught how to get the best out of their airplane as we are, every day of the week.

F-15 Wing commander

This aircraft is perfectly suited for our role with its long range radar facility and highly sophisticated fire control systems. We operate out of McCord AFB in Washington State and are one of the three ADTAC units to trade in our F-106's for the F-15A/B. Once the other Squadrons in the Command have finished refitting and ASAT is operational, we will be performing anti satellite missions as well as some of our routine patrol and interception duties.

Public Affairs Chief for 318th FIS

You bring an F-15 in easy – real easy. Early on, they found the ship a little hard to stop. Then they fitted a larger speed brake and that did it. Touchdown is around 110 to 120 knots, with the nose pitched up 12 – or 12 degrees. At 80 the nose comes down gently and you brake.

F-15 Pilot

I guess it might have had something to do with those Streak Eagle records way back in '75, when an F-15 went over 100,000 feet. Anyway, they invented this missile to knock off enemy spy satellites. Satellites! I heard that it worked, too, before the enormous cost made Congress say nix. The point is though, how many other fighters could reach that kinda height with an even chance to use that sort of missile? I think that shows you what sort of performance the F-15 has. Yeah, its expensive, but then again, what real good thing isn't these days?

US Air Force public relations

You can just stand this airplane on its tail and keep going up and up. It's a unique feeling and a very happy one when you are in a dog fight situation. No aircraft can quite do what this bird can . . . maybe the Hornet and the Flanker get close. Putting it into words is hard – you just hang there and go – there is a surge, yes . . . and the sky gets to be a much deeper blue. Clean, the F-15 easily goes Mach 1 in a climb and will do Mach 2.5 at 45,000 feet.

F-15 Pilot

DRIVE SAFELY

66

FORMS

WARNING

Understandably, Edwards Air Force Base has recorded thousands of hours on the F-15 which has had a long and intensive flight test period since July of 1972. We've found all the models a real pleasure to fly – even though we're testing to the limits and aiming to find any faults before a particular model is issued to an Air Force unit. Apart from a few glitches in maintenance downtime and some engine problems a few years back, the program has been remarkably smooth.

F-15 Flight Test Pilot, Edwards AFB

That patch? That's the 525th Tactical Fighter Squadron, known as the 'Bulldogs'. The squadron is assigned to the 36th Tac Fighter Wing here at Bitburg. We've had a squadron with that name in Germany since 1945 and flown mostly fighters since day one. With the F-15 here, we have a firm commitment to the NATO alliance. It's a great place to fly.

36th TFW pilot, Bitburg AB

Check Six – Bravo Sierra! Better. Perfect tap – right in his lethal cone. Fox two! Fox two with a Lima. Outstanding, even Sierra Hotel. Two Viper drivers at my four; bat turn to avoid airway zombies and back to fluid two. One Viper driver is fangs out – no way he can cut it – too much tiger error. Furball all over the damn sky; everyone hassling. Zero bogey dope. Gut check. OK. Situational awareness up. Check six. Knock it off and home to heaven. *(Rough translation: A USAFE F-15 pilot on exercise scores a Sidewinder 'kill' and watches F-16s dog-fighting en route back to Bitburg).*

Both the right and left engines are interchangeable . . . and 'given a following wind', my crews can swop engines in under twenty minutes!

Ground crew chief

We've had F-15s here in Holland since mid September 1978. They're always ready just in case. Last June I remember we had a renegade MiG stray into NATO airspace . . . we tracked her through to Southern Belgium where she crashed. The Flogger turned out to be without a pilot. He'd ejected back over in Poland.

USAFE Air Traffic Control Officer

At Bitburg our F-15s live in what we call Theater Air Base Vulnerability Shelters, or TAB Vs. Each fighter has one to itself and the shelters are designed to prevent blast damage in the event of Round Three happening. The jet exhaust is funneled away so that guys can work inside.

Ground crew technician

Each F-15 carries four Sparrows on each lower corner of the engine nacelles, plus up to four Nine Limas on the wing racks. To load, we have a range of vehicles to take the strain out of ordnance loading – it's not like it used to be!

F-15 Crewchief

Bear hunting is what the 57th does best. Over Iceland and the north the season never closes. Last year we bagged the highest number of Bear interceptions in one month and set a record. Mostly we take their picture and they turn back. Their crews don't respond much – but we all know the story about the F-4 back-seater who flew alongside this Bear and held up a Playboy centerfold – that sure got their attention!

Pilot, 57th Fighter Interceptor Squadron, Iceland

I recall that back in 1972 when the Eagle was new, Col Wendell Shawler was the only Air Force F-15 pilot around. After one flight he told test pilot Burrows, 'You've got a great flying machine here, Irv'. Since then we could have staffed a whole company office to handle the superlative feedback we get. Strange thing is that the pilots have not come up with a nickname, apart from 'awesome'. But 'awesome Eagle' does have a good sound.

McDonnell Douglas public relations

Not only is the F-15 a great airplane to fly, it has safety built-in – three hydraulic systems, self-sealing fuel tanks, multiple electrical systems and redundant flight controls. It gives me confidence that whenever I go out, the F-15 will most probably get me home in one piece, even if there's a major malfunction. A lot of our missions are duplicated in simulators before we leave the ground. These are so detailed, they're almost real time and as far as the Air Force is concerned, they cost about one tenth that of flying the F-15.

Air National Guard pilot

You land at 130 knots on a standard day with 30,000 pounds of weight under you. There isn't a drag chute and you have to deploy the speed brake to slow you down along with relying on the aerodynamic braking capability of the aircraft which decelerates you smoothly down.

F-15 Pilot

The F-15E is a lethal strike aircraft and multi-mission fighter. It is not dissimilar in external appearance to the B variant but internally, the avionics are far from similar. Just climbing into the cockpit confirms you're in a missionized environment – the radar that's been fitted can give precise infrared imaging up to fifty nautical miles distant at night.

F-15E pilot

All modern fighters are gut wrenching with the amount of engine power they command. It really is amazing what the human body can stand when G forces are thrown at it, especially in air combat situations . . . One of those rare sights though is the puff ball shock wave you can see as your wingman goes through Mach 1. It's a sight that never, ever fails to impress me.

F-15 Navigator

It's our good neighbor policy not to fly high noise level fighters like the F-15 at night. Even in Germany where they have the Zulu Alert scrambles, they don't go unless it's absolutely necessary. A big plus over there is the hush house to kill jet noise during ground runs. I heard that once they'd installed these at Bitburg in the 1980s, noise complaints received by the base dropped to zero.

Military Affairs Officer